A Portrait of
Helen
Steiner Rice

A Portrait of
Helen
Steiner Rice

Dr. Mary Hilaire Tavenner

1603 Capitol Ave., Suite 310 Cheyenne, Wyoming USA 82001
1-888-980-6523 | admin@urlinkpublishing.com

URLink Print and Media is committed to excellence in the publishing industry.

Book design copyright © 2022 by URLink Print and Media. All rights reserved.

Published in the United States of America

Library of Congress Control Number: 2022905449
ISBN 978-1-68486-144-6 (Paperback)
ISBN 978-1-68486-145-3 (Digital)

14.02.22

DEDICATION

To the Friends of Helen Steiner Rice, to the International Writers Association, and to all those, young and old, who appreciate Helen's legacy. Especially, this trilogy of articles is dedicated to Helen's mom, her dad, and her sister, Gertrude.

In Memory of my precious grandmothers:

Mary Alice Grady Montgomery:
June 4, 1891-December 2, 1969
(Mom's Mom)

Ena Imelda Henderson Tavenner:
March 7, 1881 – June 15, 1964
(Dad's Mom)

and the two women who were
"like a grandmother" to me:

Sister M. Borgia Schorer, OSF:
July 14, 1892 – May 7, 1995
(Syracuse Franciscan Nun)

Mrs. Alethea (Miss Allie) Smith:
December 24, 1905 – April 1, 2000
(Rosalynn Carter's Mother)

And to Helen, "A Pen in the Hand of God".

Editor: Anne Somplack
Readers: Andrea Dunn and Linda Mathewson
Copyright: 2021 Dutch Ink Publishing, Lorain, OH

CONTENTS

PREFACE

This booklet was written for the sole purpose of teaching people about Helen Steiner Rice. It was originally composed to be published in a Lorain area newspaper, but that did not happen. Permission is granted by the author to use this text for educational purposes. I suggest that you give "your students/audience" the 20 question "pre-test" to see how much they may already know about Mrs. Rice and her legacy before you teach or speak. After reading or teaching the three articles, the educator may wish to give the same twenty-question quiz as a "post-test". Please cite the author's name and source when using these articles.. It is hoped these stories will be used as a springboard for further relevant and inspirational studies and celebrations of Helen, her life journey, her God-given gift for poetry, for loving those all souls who were substantial relationships throughout her life, and for her extraordinary degree of faith in Her (and Our) Creator.

PART ONE:

The Life Journey of Helen Steiner Rice

HELEN STEINER RICE

How Much Do You Know?

It is amazing that so few people know very much about Helen Steiner Rice, (especially in her hometown), a literary giant who continues to impact the hearts and minds of millions throughout the world! Helen came from humble beginnings, yet attained a "greatness" of accomplishments which few of us will ever reach in life. Helen was born in Lorain, Ohio, graduated from Lorain High School, and is buried in the town she so dearly loved.

How much do you know actually about her? Below is a twenty-question quiz. Subtract five points for every incorrect answer. Anyone scoring, less than 100 percent, will likely benefit from reading the following facts and stories about Helen Steiner Rice, Poet Laureate.

Multiple Choice: Circle the answers you believe are true.

BE CAREFUL—*Sometimes, there is more than one correct answer!*

1. Helen Steiner Rice is buried in
    a. Ridge Hill Cemetery.
    b. Calvary.
    c. Elmwood Cemetery.

2. Helen's only sister was
   a. Ellen.
   b. Gertrude.
   c. Catherine.

3. Growing up in Lorain, Helen always wanted to be:
   a. A lawyer.
   b. A preacher.
   c. A congresswoman.
   d. All of the above.

4. The following statement or statements are true of Helen:
   a. Helen loved taking photographs.
   b. Helen's first job was at the Lorain Board of Health.
   c. Helen was a bookkeeper, but enjoyed decorating lamp shades more.
   d. All of the above.

5. The following statement or statements are true of Helen:
   a. Helen was a tall, thin woman.
   b. Helen was invited to the White House and was photographed with President Coolidge.
   c. Helen founded her own speaker's bureau.
   d. All of the above.

6. The following statement or statements are true of Helen's husband:
   a. His name was Jeffrey Rice.
   b. Helen met her husband when giving a speech in New York.

    c.   Helen's husband was a wealthy bank vide-president.

    d.   All of the above.

7.   The following statement or statements are true of Helen's husband
   a.   She married her husband in New York's historic Marble Collegiate Church in 1929.
   b.   They honeymooned on a cruise in the Caribbean.
   c.   After three years of marriage, her husband committed suicide.
   d.   All of the above.

8.   Helen worked for
   a.   Hallmark Greeting Cards, Inc.
   b.   American Greeting Cards.
   c.   Gibson Greeting Cards.

9.   The following statement or statements are true of Helen's family:
   a.   Her father died in 1918 in the Spanish Influenza epidemic.
   b.   Her mother died in1945 from a heart attack.
   c.   Her sister died in 1992 from an acute cerebral vascular accident in Lorain.
   d.   All of the above.

10. The following statement or statements are true of Helen:
   a.   Helen could not swim and refused to take cruises because her cousin died in a fire while on a cruise vacation.

    b.   Helen's poetry received national exposure when read on the Lawrence Welk show in 1960.

    c.   Helen likely may have written as many as two million poems.

    d.   All of the above.

11. The following statement or statements are true of Helen:
    a.   Helen was a fervent Presbyterian.
    b.   Helen did not attend church.
    c.   Helen was a fervent Methodist.
    d.   Helen converted to Catholicism after her husband died.

12. The following statement or statements are true of Helen:
    a.   At times, Helen was a political activist.
    b.   The top selling Christmas card in 1964 was Helen's "Praying Hands" card, selling over one and a half million copies.
    c.   Helen lived in a hotel most of her life.
    d.   All of the above.

13. The following statement or statements are true of Helen:
    a.   In 1961, Helen "officially, retired after nearly forty years as an editor.
    b.   Helen did not believe in retirement and stayed on the payroll at American Greeting until just before her death in 1980.
    c.   Helen suffered from depression and melancholy.
    d.   All of the above.

14. The following statement or statements are true of Helen:
    a. Her husband died in a Cincinnati train accident.
    b. Helen retired from "public speaking" after her husband's death.
    c. By 1980, sales of her cards topped 75 million and her books surpassed sales of 2 million.
    d. All of the above.

15. The following statement or statements are true of Helen:
    a. Helen died in a Catholic nursing home in Cleveland.
    b. Helen wanted to die in a Methodist nursing home in Cincinnati.
    c. When Helen died, among those sending messaged were John Paul II and Rosalyn and Jimmy Carter.
    d. All of the above.

16. The following statement or statements are true of Helen:
    a. The only college degree Helen ever received was an Honorary Doctorate of Humane Letters from the Sisters of Charity at Mt. St. Joseph College in Cincinnati, OH.
    b. Helen loved to write, but she very much disliked to read.
    c. Helen left her personal effects to her only sister and most of her financial wealth to her Foundation.
    d. All of the above.

17. Grants used to be available in memory of Helen from:
    a. The Helen Steiner Rice Foundation of Cincinnati.
    b. The Red Cross.
    c. The Lorain Historical Society.

18. The following statement or statements are true of Helen:
    a. Helen estimated that she may have written as many as two million poems during her lifetime.
    b. *In the Vineyard of the Lord* is Helen's *only* published biographical resource.
    c. Helen would ALWAYS spoke lovingly of her hometown, Lorain, Ohio.
    d. All of the above.

19. The Friends of Helen Steiner Rice was a society:
    a. That boasted nearly a thousand members after only five years!
    b. That raised the money needed to help pay for a Lorain Public School to be named in honor of Helen Steiner Rice.
    c. Established to memorialize Helen in her hometown and to educate the public about her life.
    d. All of the above.

20. Helen Steiner Rice is probably most remembered for
    a. Her Poetry.
    b. Her flair for hats, purses and style of dress.
    c. Her unwavering faith in God.
    d. All of the above *and ever so much, much more!*

Answers to the Helen Steiner Rice
Twenty-Question Quiz:

1. c
2. b
3. d
4. a & c
5. b & c
6. c
7. d
8. c
9. d
10. b & c

11. c
12. d
13. c
14. c
15. c
16. a & c
17. a
18. a & c
19. c
20. d

HELEN STEINER RICE

[The Early Years]

It is amazing that so few Lorainites know very much about Helen Steiner Rice, a local celebrity who has touched the lives of people throughout the world. Helen came from humble beginnings, yet attained a greatness few of us seldom ever reach. The first part of this book is three articles I have composed about Helen Steiner Rice, once nicknamed the "Lorain Tornado" for the energy with which she shared her gifts for public speaking, her gift for poetry and for motivating others. I first published this book twenty years after Helen died, in 2001. I am republishing it this year, 2021 because 40 years ago, on April 23, this precious and gifted soul entered eternity. The second part of this biography will update much that has happened over the past twenty years. I will begin by sharing circumstances of Helen's early years.

Life in Lorain

Both of Helen's parents were born on farms near Wooster, Ohio, in 1892: Anna Bieri and John Steiner. Anna Bieri's family had emigrated from Switzerland and John's family came from Germany. Their families settled in Sterling, not far from Wooster. When John took a job with the Baltimore and Railway, they married then moved to Lorain, renting a home on Lexington Avenue. Helen Elaine Steiner was born on May 19, 1900. Her only sister, Gertrude, was born a year and a half later, on November 2, 1902.

The Steiner family worshipped at the Twentieth Street Methodist Church, where Helen developed a fervent faith in God. Helen's maternal grandmother taught Helen a love for poetry and Scripture, and helped to develop her natural tendencies toward kindness and understanding. Helen attended Garden Avenue School until the family moved to 2714 Reid Avenue, where Mr. Steiner had a house built for his family. Helen then attended Garfield and later, graduated from Lorain High School in 1918.

As a youngster Helen dreamed of being a preacher, and she was an excellent Bible School teacher for her Methodist Church congregation. In high school she published poems in the Lorain Scimitar in both 1916 and 1918. Then Helen's ambitions changed. She then hoped to study liberal arts at Ohio Wesleyan and onto law at Ohio State.

After graduating, (Lorain High School, Class A), Helen began her first job at Lorain Electric Light and Power Company. Only months later, her father fell victim to the worldwide Spanish influenza epidemic of 1918. He died at the age of forty-six and was buried at Elmwood Cemetery.

College was now out of the question and Helen resolved to earn an income for her mother and sister. She wanted to decorate the office windows at the Power Company and she did. Her boss, Mr. Quillin, asked Helen if she would like to learn how to decorate lamp shades. In turn, Helen was to teach other women how to decorate them, and consequently more of the public would, hopefully, be encouraged to use electricity for lighting their respective homes (instead of gas or any other means). Helen was delighted to use her creative skills in the workplace and eagerly and successful set forth her plans to promote the Lorain Electric Light and Power Company.

She was even sent to Cleveland where she learned the "art" of making silk lamp shades and used her poetry skills to write advertisements. Helen was soon promoted to "advertising manager", and she received several prizes as well as opportunities to travel and speak around the country. She found herself in sales and learned bookkeeping as well while working for Mr. Quillin. All of this only honed her skills for both business and creativity.

A Successful Businesswoman and Feminist

As a young woman, Helen had a flair for fashion: perhaps influenced because her mother had been a talented seamstress. She also enjoyed taking photographs and being photographed. In 1924, Lorain was struck by a very destructive tornado. (In truth, it was the deadliest ever recorded in Ohio—with 81 recorded deaths.) Still, Helen was nicknamed the "Lorain Tornado" because of her unbridled enthusiasm and optimism as a public speaker! During her many presentations Helen especially promoted what she considered "the all-important role women play in business." She saw women as "partners" in the workplace, not merely "decorations."

In an interview she gave Donald T. Kauffman, Helen stated that women's rights were one of the many important topics she wanted to address during her public speaking career. "Women's rights were a constant topic while I was growing up; all my teachers had been suffragettes, and I firmly believe in the right and ability of women to win their own way in the world."

Helen was not much taller than five feet, but by the age of twenty-five she was already a nationally known speaker. She promoted the virtues of the public service industry and consistently advocated the advancement of women in the workplace. For the next five years, Helen crisscrossed the country in her role as one of the most popular and persuasive speakers in the public service industry. She was even invited to the White House and photographed with then, President Coolidge!

Years later Helen stated, "In my many years of working among women, I have observed that every woman who rose to any great success attained her goal through her ability to get along with other women; when you hear a woman say that she wouldn't work for another women for a million dollars, you are listening to the most efficient little grave digger in the world. She is not only digging her own grave, but she is burying all the rest of us with her. If a woman has the brains to work herself into an executive position, boost for her...help her climb still higher! For every time she goes up a step, she leaves a vacancy to be filled by you...if you've shown yourself worthy. The women who go up are those who are sincerely interested in work and who work with their own sex."

Helen continues, "Unless women go up as a sex, you do not go up! At least, you do not go up to stay; as long as some women are underpaid and unrecognized you will be underpaid and unrecognized also. The line is not drawn between trades and businesses; it is drawn distinctly and firmly between men and women!"

During the Spring of 1927, Helen founded her own speaker's bureau. She operated "Steiner Service" out of Lorain. She had decided to strike out on her own because of many scandals, occurring at that time, in "public utilities."

Her Knight in Shining Armor

In June of 1928, Helen spoke at a bankers' convention in Dayton, Ohio. She agreed to her fee of $150.00, plus expenses. (Today, that could be as much as $150,000 or more!) Mr. Franklin Rice, Vice-President of his Dayton Saving Bank, a bachelor, was assigned to escort Helen; after her talk, they dined together and Mr. Rice agreed to send Helen any newspaper clippings about her speech the following day. Helen remarked that she "usually received front page coverage." A few days later, the wealthy bank officer, Mr. Rice, personally delivered the front page newspaper article to Lorain in a chauffeur-driven limousine!

Mr. Franklin Rice had been a trained aviator during World War I, but the war ended before he ever saw action. After the war, banks prospered and Franklin then earned his prestigious position as Vice President of Dayton Savings and Trust.

Three months after their first meeting, Franklin chartered a yacht to take Helen and her sister on a Lake Erie cruise. Two months after that, the two were engaged. Helen and Franklin formally announced their intentions to marry at a bridge party given in Helen's honor December 5, 1928.

Near the time of their wedding, Franklin's brother, Elwood, insisted on planning and hosting an elegant dinner at the Plaza Hotel in New York City, where Elwood E. Rice had reserved a drawing room and suite. Only Helen's sister, Gertrude, and fourteen other guests attended the exclusive repast.

Helen and Franklin's elegant wedding took place on January 30, 1929, in the drawing room of Elwood's apartment at the Plaza Hotel. Rev. Daniel A. Poling, pastor of the Marble Collegiate Church, NY, officiated. Thus, Helen was not married in her hometown or even in her home church "as was customary back in her day".

By noon, after their wedding day, the couple boarded the *S. S. Columbus*, bound for their anticipated honeymoon cruise in the Caribbean. They enjoyed every comfort, yet Helen was troubled by the poverty and squalor she saw, for her first time, while in Trinidad, Cuba, and Panama. Still, their adventure meant so much to her that she saved every bit of her honeymoon memorabilia! (Some of which is currently housed in the Lorain Historical Society.)

After their Caribbean adventures, the delightfully happy couple moved into their fourteen-room home at 713 West Grand Avenue in Dayton, OH. Helen luxuriated at the impressive and large estate, complete with three expensive cars. The two looked forward to a long and prosperous life together, but fate would dictate otherwise.

HELEN STEINER RICE

[The Middle Years]

Married Life

As previously stated, in 1929, Helen Elaine Steiner married Franklin Dryden Rice, a very wealthy bank vice president from Dayton. They had met only six months earlier and, after a Caribbean honeymoon, the couple settled in their 713 West Grand Avenue home in Dayton.

Franklin had invested a major share of their assets in the stock market and was not concerned when it began to fluctuate. Helen suggested he stop buying the securities, but Franklin chose not to heed her advice. He thought the fluctuations were only "a temporary aberration". It wasn't. In October of 1929, the U.S. stock market crashed, precipitating the Great Depression. By December, the Rices' net worth fell to less than two dollars. They now owed money for groceries, coal, insurance, travel and clothing. Many banks were in utter collapse, and like so many other Americans, Franklin lost his job at Dayton Savings and Trust.

Franklin's brother, Elwood, was able to assume their house mortgage at $100.00 a month. Still, Helen preferred to be independent of his offers of help and went back to the speaker's circuit she had known for the past five years. She also earned money by teaching the card rules of "Bridge" to others. Elwood insisted that Helen and her husband keep up an appearance of financial well-being. Despite Helen's objections, Franklin agreed to do exactly that. In whatever way possible, Helen's mother stepped up to help them as well.

In October of 1931, Helen had established strong ties with JR Gibson of the Gibson Art Company of Cincinnati, with the help of Sam Heed, a man she had met in Los Angeles during one of her many talks. By mid-December, Helen had accepted a full-time position with Gibson. This meant that she would need to live at the Gibson Hotel in Cincinnati and visit her husband, Franklin, on weekends.

Franklin has refused to sell their home in Dayton, so "weekends in Dayton" was something of a mutual compromise. Franklin could not secure an income at the time and despaired over not being able to support his household. To compound matters, in May of 1932, he was named in a lawsuit that accused a brokerage house that Franklin had dealt with, of making illegal transactions. The scandal was local front-page news. Franklin was understandably overwhelmed by these devastating circumstances.

A Much Greater Loss

In her autobiography, *In the Vineyard of the Lord*, Helen wrote, "Then one day I come home from playing bridge with some of the ladies at the club and learned the horrible news—Franklin had gone to the garage, closed the door, started one of the cars, and died of carbon monoxide poisoning." Franklin died on October 14, 1932. He and Helen had been married almost three years.

Franklin's suicide letter asked Helen to repay the money her mother had loaned them to help support his mother during the remainder of her life. He did not want to be pitied. His letter read, in part: "I have often told you that I was not going to go down, and down and down and become a common bum, and I won't either. When my money goes, which it had, I too, must fade out of the picture, as I must go down with the colors at the top of the mast, and the band playing. No one up until now knows the terrible hard conditions under which I had been trying to get along, trading this for that and switching this into that to get money, just to live from day to day. The most enjoyable time of my life had been the weekends that I had to look forward to, with you, and how I did enjoy them! Darling, I love you more than anything and hope this one last error I am committing will be forgiven...."

Franklin was buried in the cemetery of Zion Memorial Church in Moraine, Ohio. Their home and most of their possessions, except those Helen had taken to Cincinnati, were sold at auction to defray their staggering debts. Helen threw herself into her work at the Gibson Art Company. When Ethel Brainerd, editor of the Gibson card lines, died suddenly, Helen assumed this position.

Helen had a great capacity for loyalty and friendship and made many wonderful friends at Gibson. Throughout the 1930s, she wrote verses rich with her humor, talent for rhyme, and clever wit. She became politically active in the city council race of Willis D. Gradison, often helping him to write his speeches. She endeared herself to his family and worked closely with Willis. She and Willis both worked together while trying to bring some relief to the victims of the Cincinnati "Great Flood" of 1937.

Meanwhile, Sam Heed and his wife continued to be invaluable friends. In 1938, Helen joined them on a cruise upon the Mediterranean Sea.

The Recognition, Yet More Sorrow

By 1940, Helen Steiner Rice was already widely acknowledged as one of the leading poets in the greeting card industry. As editor, she composed verses and approved the work of her staff and their freelance writers. During World War II, under Helen's direction, the Gibson greeting cards capitalized on patriotic themes of inspiring verse.

Throughout her life, Helen had a great love for reading, which contributed to the breadth of her rich variety of topics and themes.

She now demonstrated even a keener sense of humor and insights into life. Helen possessed a most vivacious personality. She developed a reputation for her impeccable attire and, at any gathering, "The lady of the Hats" did not go unnoticed. Her gloves, beautiful purses, and fancy hats were "practically trademark".

In February of 1945, Helen's mother, Anna, died suddenly of a heart attack. Helen was almost forty-five years of age. Her mother had pre-arranged her funeral service and had written her own death notice in an effort to spare her daughters this difficult task. Helen's devotion to her mother and sister was always remarkable, but the loving bond she shared with Gertrude grew even more profound with their mother's passing. The two women shared every holiday together and wrote to each other daily. Helen, obviously, made countless trips to Lorain from Cincinnati.

Not even Helen could imagine the personal success she would enjoy in the years to come. She would soon receive national attention and become a celebrity worthy of both a President's and a Pope's attention—but not without a price.

HELEN STEINER RICE

[The Later Years]

The Gibson Hotel

Helen Steiner Rice lived in the same hotel room on Fifth Street in downtown Cincinnati ever since she began to work at the Gibson Art Company. The people employed at her hotel were like family to Helen. For most of those years while at Gibson, Ida Ginn was the maid who cleaned her room; Helen called her "Mom." Helen was also close friends with the maintenance supervisor, the elevator operator, and those who worked at the Gibson's Sidewalk Café.

In her fifties, Helen began to experience some serious health problems, yet she still remained cheerful and accepting. Giving spiritual counsel and compassion through her poetry and letter writing morphed into a kind of "personal ministry". Her yearly Christmas greeting card verses came forth and they were one masterpiece after another.

In time, Helen came to believe that the solution to the world's problems lay not in technology or institutional religion, but in spreading the eternal message of love. She believed that God wanted her to be an example of how loving behavior could be a part of our everyday life.

National Exposure

At the age of sixty, Helen watched as Aladdin Pallante, a performer on the Lawrence Welk Show, read her verse, "The Priceless Gift of Christmas." The following year he read her poem "The Praying Hands" during the Thanksgiving special. By 1962, her "Inspirational Verses" were becoming big business. In 1963, just after the assassination of President Kennedy, the Lawrence Welk show featured her poem, "Tribute to JFK." It, too, became another extraordinary success.

During the 1960s Helen's popularity soared and people flocked to buy her books of poetry, to get her autograph, and to meet her. She felt the pain of lost privacy and the need for others to transact with a celebrated author. The pain she experienced is the pain that often comes from such notoriety. These were years of great public recognition and appreciation from her fans. She received hoards of letters. Her personal secretary, Mary Jo Eling, was an immense help, but Helen became increasingly exhausted and suffered pangs of discouragement as she tried to respond to the many letters and her immense popularity.

During this time, Helen had an encounter with CIT Financial, the company that had acquired Gibson Greeting in 1964. She also battled with Doubleday over copyright privileges. Despite those difficulties, her first hardcover book was published in 1967. *Just for You* was a tremendous success and her advance royalty check was shared with Christ Methodist Church in Lorain and Wesley Chapel in Cincinnati.

Helen chose Revell Publishing for her second hardcover, *Heart Gifts,* printed in November of 1968. Again, her royalties were sent to her churches in Lorain and Cincinnati. Helen was devastated when she learned Proctor and Gamble had acquired the Wesley Chapel property for expansion and that the 175-year-old church she dearly loved would be demolished.

In her seventies, Helen suffered from arthritis and a deteriorating spinal condition. In 1971, after nearly forty years of dedicated service, Helen officially retired as editor at Gibson, but she decided to remain affiliated as consultant and retain an office there. This allowed her to continue to work with Mary Jo Eling as they attempted to answer her volumes of correspondence. She insisted, "I go there every day, but I'm working for God now, not for Gibson."

Depression

October, the month of her father's and husband's deaths, was always particularly difficult for Helen. Her memories of them plunged her into a seasonal depression each year. In time, these melancholy periods intensified and Helen began to mistrust her own sincerity of purpose.

When Helen was seventy-five, the aging Gibson Hotel, her home for nearly forty years, was razed. She and all the other residents were told they must leave. A friend arranged for her to move into a suite at the Cincinnati Club, a residential hotel not far from the Gibson, but the inconvenience depleted Helen psychologically and physically. Her rib cage slipped over her right lung, cutting off most of her oxygen supply, resulting in heart complications. Depressed, short of breath, and limited in mobility, Helen lost thirty pounds because of the move. Some of the discs in her back deteriorated further and she was hospitalized. She now needed to wear a back brace.

After producing numerous best sellers, Helen agrees to give Fred Bauer, the editor of *Guidepost*s a series of interviews about her memories and philosophy. The product of these interviews, called *In the Vineyard of the Lord*, became Helen Steiner Rice's only autobiographical book resource.

Her Charitable Foundation, a Final Honor, and Her Death

Shortly thereafter, in 1979, a son of her dear friend, Willis Gradison Sr., introduced Helen to a Cincinnati attorney, Eugene Ruehmann, who specialized in estate planning. It was her dear friend, Fred Bauer, who had encouraged Helen to establish a Foundation so that her sizeable estate would be used to help the poor, the sick, and the needy.

Helen's Will stipulated that her household, jewelry, and all other such personal belongings be left to her sister, Gertrude M. Steiner, or to Gertrude's lineal descendants. At the time of Helen's death, her sister, Gertrude, was still living in Lorain. Gertrude died twelve years after Helen, on March 9, 1992, at the age of ninety—leaving many personal assets to her husband, Lambert Fitzgerald.

On April 23, 1980, Helen fell and broke her left hip and waist. After a hospital stay, she was transferred to the Franciscan Terrace Nursing Home in Wyoming, a Northern suburb of Cincinnati. Good wishes were sent by President and Mrs. Jimmy Carter, Pope John Paul II, and many, many others.

Helen Steiner Rice had given up her dreams of college to earn income for her family, but on March 14, 1981, in a private ceremony at the Franciscan Terrace Nursing Home, the president of Mt. St. Joseph College, Sr. Jean Patrice Harrington, and A Saint Elizabeth Ann Seton Sister of Charity presented Helen with an Honorary Doctorate of Humane Letters.

Helen died on a Thursday evening, April 23, 1981 at the age of eighty. Helen was buried next to her parents at Elmwood Cemetery in Lorain. At her death, she had twenty-three major publications to her credit in addition to countless card verses, both signed and unsigned.

Although, even after 40 years, there are far too few Lorainites who know much about their hometown fan and celebrity, Helen always held the city close to her heart. She frequently told people that a goodly share of her early education and encouragement came from the people of Lorain. She wrote to a friend, "Although I have been away from Lorain for over twenty-five years, I still have a warm feeling of fondness and gratitude in my heart for the spot <u>I am still proud to call **my hometown.**</u>"

Helen Steiner Rice's 10 Commandments

As you can see, the personal commandments of
Helen Steiner Rice emphasize optimism!

1. Thou shalt be happy.
2. Thou shalt use thy talents to make others glad.
3. Thou shalt rise above defeat and trouble.
4. Thou shalt look upon each day as a new day.
5. Thou shalt always do they best and leave the rest to God.
6. Thou shalt not waste thy time and energy in useless worry.
7. Thou shalt look only on the bright side of life.
8. Thou shalt not be afraid of tomorrow.
9. Thou shalt have a kind word and a kind deed for everyone.
10. Thou shalt say each morning, "I am a child of God and nothing can hurt me."

PART TWO

My "30" Year Journey with Helen Steiner Rice

HOW I GOT INVOLVED

I am Dr. Mary Hilaire (Sally) Tavenner. I, too, share a passion for recording words. My Doctorate is from the University of South Florida in Tampa, and the Ph.D. is in Reading/Language Arts. I have taught "about" 2,000 children and "about" 1,000 adults throughout my 46 year-long teaching career. I was born in Lorain, OH. In fact my mother was pregnant with me when she moved into the house on the corner of Alexander Ave. and D Street. My Grandmother, Ena Imelda Tavenner, bought 304 Alexander in 1945…from Daisy Henry, "surrogate" aunt to my beloved second grade teacher, Daisy Pivacek Rich. (Mrs. Pivacek Rich was, I believe, my predominant inspiration to "**become a teacher** *when I grew up*".)

At the age of 17, after graduating from Lorain High School, I moved to Syracuse, NY and became a Syracuse Franciscan Religious Sister. I lived and taught in New York State for about 15 years, teaching in Catholic Schools in Syracuse, Albany and Fulton for 12 years. Then, I was "assigned" to teach in Lorain, at St. Anthony of Padua School, which is about a block from the Lorain/Tavenner family homestead at 304 Alexander Ave. in Lorain.

In 1985, I was sent to Tampa, Florida to teach with other Syracuse Franciscan Sisters, for a year. After that year in Tampa, I was sent to Puerto Rico to teach, but I had such poor command of Spanish, that I could not imagine living in a Spanish speaking nation. I pleaded to go to an English speaking mission. However, our vow of obedience was a factor and I went, as assigned. After 3 months, I left the community and returned to Tampa.

Having earned my Bachelor's in Education from Catholic University and my Master's in Religious Studies from St. Charles Seminary in Philadelphia, I wanted even more education.

I had desired a Ph.D. and decided Tampa was "the place" to earn it. I lived a 15 minute commute from the University of South Florida. For six years, I would attend evening classes after teaching during the day, and spent another two years doing research for USF, while teaching classes for them for a nominal fee. Nearing the end of my Dissertation Requirements, I received a phone call from my mother's Physician in Lorain. He told me that Mother, (who had both serious COPD and emphysema), had "about 6 months" to live. Her Medical Doctor wanted my mother to move into a local nursing home.

Mom and Dad had raised 7 awesome kids. No way would I tell Mom what her doctor had just told me. Nor did I tell my siblings. Instead, I called Mother and asked if I might move back to Lorain to live with her. The University members on my Doctoral Committee were very upset to see me leaving the program, after almost 8 years of intense effort and <u>before</u> completing the necessary requirements for completion.

Mom was more than eager to for me to return. Maybe her Physician had even asked her to enter a nursing home. I do not know for sure. That is rarely on anyone's list of "something I would like to do". As it turned out, after I quit teaching for USF, I could not sell my condo. It took me six months to finally secure a sale! And in that time, I devoted every day to finishing and defending both my research and dissertation. With God's grace, I was successful. I moved home and returned to Tampa later that year (1993) to attend my graduation ceremony and to unite with friends I had made during those ten years in Tampa. (Before I moved back to Ohio, I held a "graduation celebration" for my friends and support group while living in Florida. The lot of us, and even my brother, Bob, had flown down from Ohio to be there **for me.** Bob always made an effort to "be there for anyone he ever loved."

Mom was so pleased that I was coming, as was everyone else. No nursing home for Mother! I was totally welcomed home, and family helped me to move back into "304". It was great fun to be back with Mom, neighbors, cousins and family, on every level. After ten years in Florida, there were some adjustments, but the transition was exceptional.

One thing that did come to mystify me was that so many people in my hometown of Lorain did not seem to know that Helen Steiner Rice was a Lorainite! Helen was born here and is buried here in our city cemetery, Elmwood, along with her sister, Gertrude, and their parents. This actually bothered me: that a poet, so well loved and well known in both New York State and in Florida was not "known in her hometown!" The New York Times had named Helen "Poet Laureate of the Greeting Card World" yet she was barely known here…city of her birth and burial! Even my mother owned some books of her poetry and I was somewhat familiar with her life…but could not understand these circumstances. Some residents had heard of Helen, maybe even knew she was an extremely talented poet…but still, most had no idea that she was **one of us**! This struck me as strange, and I would frequently express such thoughts during conversation.

"THE FAITH FOLLOWERS"

Elnora Perdew Alferio, a retired teacher and friend to my mother, lived just across the street from our home. Elnora suggested to me that I join "The Faith Followers". In 1988, Helen Meyers established the group only seven years after Helen Steiner Rice had died, as Helen Meyers wanted this prominent and greatly accomplished talent to be recognized for her most generous spirit and many accomplishments. On Helen Steiner Rice's birthday, May 19th, Helen Meyers asked her group to attend a prayer service at Helen's grave each year on May 19th. Her growing society, met in First Methodist Church, on the corner of Reid and 6th St. in Lorain.

This was not Helen Steiner Rice's Methodist Congregation. Originally, Helen worshipped with her family at 20th Street Methodist Church, now demolished. The founder of "Faith Followers", Helen Meyers, had also prayed at 20th Street Methodist Church and even back then, held high esteem, respect and even love for Helen Steiner. Helen Meyers died the year before I returned to Lorain, so I never knew her, but I was very happy to know that Mrs. Meyers had shared a similar passion for Mrs. Rice. So, I went to the church, as Elnora suggested "to investigate" as to what they were doing to keep the memory of HSR alive. I was very happy to sense good intent and collective effort.

Minerva Pignatella was their President when I joined. I think it was the second meeting that I attended, when I was elected to serve as the "Faith Followers Vice-President". I spent much of the next five years finding, for their group, speakers and arranging various programs. Our meetings were always a luncheon along with some entertainment. I did whatever Minerva, membership, Elmer Meyers or his new wife, Nancy, would ask of me. They were a very pleasant social group. Being back in Lorain, after ten years away, I was grateful to establish and build some new relationships. My mother was happy to see me helping them as well.

One day, when I was giving a talk on Helen's life for the Lorain Historical Society, Lambert Fitzgerald was in my audience. After the talk, I met Lambert Gertie's husband) and immediately sensed him to be a very pleasant man. I asked if we could share some time together, and get to know each other. He gave me his phone number and asked me to call him. It was almost a year later before I decided to call. Lambert invited me to lunch and then, after our lunch, to his lovely home in Amherst. While at his house, Lambert proceeded to show me his treasure trove of HSR memorabilia: letters, photographs, etc.

When I saw a particular portrait of HSR, I was smitten! Lambert could tell, and insisted that I accept the portrait! (The image is on the cover of this book.) I named this particular likeness "The Lorain Portrait" in honor of a city that so needed to be proud of Helen and her God-given talents. I sensed that this portrait was priceless and continued to insist that he not just give it to me. Lambert put it in my hands and told me that he wanted me to absolutely have it. I, MOST gratefully, accepted his magnanimous gift. This is still, almost 20 years later, among my most-treasured of possessions! Lambert and I have remained good friends, ever since that day together. I think very highly of him.

Most of Lorain did not know that Lambert had married Helen's sister, Gertrude. They had eloped to Kentucky, in secret, but many good things came of the marriage! He was 30 or more years younger than Gertie, but they had a mutual loving and giving relationship with each other. Lambert would gladly help Gertie with various tasks, and they would even travel internationally together. They lived next door to each other (Lambert rented a room at the Blaedorn Residence) for a number of years. After Helen died, Gertie appreciated Lambert all the more. They had truly become the very best of friends!

As my friendship grew with Lambert, I could sense his profound and painful grief after she had died. (It was the year before I returned to Lorain.) Gert had received all of Helen's personal effects after her only sister, and dearest friend had died in Wyoming, (suburb of Cincinnati, Ohio) in a Catholic Nursing home, on April 23, 1981. Now, when Gertrude died, these many treasures, and very personal belongings of Helen's had then been safely entrusted to the care of Lambert. However, Helen's fiscal estate of approximately a million dollars or so was entrusted to the care of Eugene Ruehlmann, a lawyer she knew. Mr. Ruehlmann was in the process of establishing Helen's sizeable estate into a "trust fund". The lawyer and his wife, pretty much would now decide how Helen's money would be distributed.

A NEW PRESIDENT FOR FAITH FOLLOWERS

———————•◎◉◎•———————

When Minerva resigned as President of the Faith Followers, because her husband had serious health issues, the membership elected me as their new President. As President of Faith Followers, I ordered pens, advertising our group and I paid for them. Jean Cook, Nancy Meyers and a few others were very upset that I did this without asking their permission. I had no idea this marketing strategy would make them so very unhappy with me. They told me, "You may be President, but you do not make any decisions without our approval." I felt like I was being scolded for doing a good deed. It made me very uncomfortable and thought, "The writing was on the wall."

In February of 1999, my mother had died and I had even more time to devote my time and resources to Lorain's legacy of Helen Steiner Rice. And, by now, I had met both Dick and Betty Knitter at several Helen Steiner Rice events. I often gave talks locally on HSR's life. Both Dick and Betty clearly had a genuine and loving respect for both Helen Steiner Rice and for Helen Meyers; the Founder of the Faith Followers. The more the three of us shared time and conversations together, the more we found each other on "a very similar page" regarding many HSR and "Faith Follower" issues. They both also thought highly of Lambert Fitzgerald. Consequently, we planned to meet at the Knitter home on December 12, 1999 with the intention of establishing "The Friends of Helen Steiner Rice".

And that was exactly what we did do that very day. At this time, I want to just share the history of a this group the four of us established in our collaborative efforts to share the legacy of Mrs. Rice, especially in Lorain, where, still, so few residents really knew much, if anything of Helen.

HISTORY OF THE "FRIENDS OF HELEN STEINER RICE"

On Sunday afternoon, December 12, 1999, four people met at the home of Dick and Betty Knitter. Dr. Mary Hilaire Tavenner and Mr. Lambert Fitzgerald (brother-in-law of Helen Steiner Rice) joined the Knitters in their living room, "for the purpose of establishing a society meant to educate the public and to promote the life of Helen Steiner Rice". We were there to recognize the world-wide, inspirational impact of Helen's prolific and impactful life and her God-given talent for poetry. These same four people did not feel enough was being done in her hometown of Lorain to acknowledge Helen's positive and profound influence of her life.

The four agreed to assume the following roles of leadership for this additional Lorain Helen S. Rice society: President: Dr. Mary Hilaire Tavenner; Vice-President: Lambert Fitzgerald; Secretary: Betty Knitter, and Treasurer: Dick Knitter. In time, both Betty (2005) and Dick (2006) Knitter died and Lambert respectfully resigned, with other interests and personal responsibilities. Dr. Tavenner (for about six years had served as Vice-President and President for the "Faith Followers", now completely disbanded and dissolved. Dr. Tavenner continued to serve as President of the "Friends of Helen Steiner Rice" for seven years until major changes came about. It is very sad that the "Faith Follower" leadership" did not see "The Friends of Helen

Steiner" as an "additional source" of educating and promulgating the talents and legacy of Helen Steiner Rice!

One of the more relevant things Dr. Tavenner was able to accomplish as President of the Faith Followers was to approach the Mayor of Lorain, Mayor Kozouria, and requested 3 street signs to be placed near the grave of Helen and on North Ridge Road, travelling both east and west of the furthest west entrance to Elmwood Cemetery. Dr. Tavenner designed this street sign, obtained a logo for the Faith Followers, bought and paid for advertising pens and paid for them, so they may be distributed to advertise the Faith Followers to the public.

The last official thing I did as president was another of my ideas…to oversee the placement and dedication of those three signs in the spring of 2000, before handing in my resignation to the Faith Followers in June of 2000. It was all just too painful for so much personal effort and work to serve the HSR cause.

On November 1, 2001, the Friends of Helen Steiner Rice held a fundraiser at the downtown, Broadway, historic "Palace Theater." The "Saints Day Concert with Tom Franzak" was not well attended and consequently, we found ourselves $2000.00 in debt, so I personally paid, out of my pocket, the $2000.00 fee we owed for Mr. Franzak's "fund raising" concert. Our treasury and ticket sales paid the other expenses such as the $500.00 for renting the Palace for the one day concert, the printing of tickets, publicity, etc. We took on a project bigger than we were!

In 2001, thanks to the initiate of Dick and Betty Knitter, we received a non-profit corporation status in the State of Ohio on January 9 of 2001 from then Ohio Secretary of State, Ken Blackwell, on January 9, 2001. (Charter number: 1206110). Only five years later, in 2006, the status was renewed, but now I became the appointed agent of the Friends of Helen Steiner Rice, after my two dear friends, both of the Knitters had died. [Richard E. (Dick) Knitter: March 22, 1927-May 20, 2006 and Betty Jean Klaue Knitter: July 24, 1928-October 11, 2005.]

In 2002, I applied for an <u>Ohio Bicentennial Marker</u> (1803-2003) for Lorain to commemorate HSR. We asked the Mayor and City Council for permission to plant the historical marker in the west section of Lakeview Park, near the Rotary Pavilion. I composed the text on the marker and my wording received approval by the Ohio History Society Committee in Columbus. I then added the HSR image that I have named, "The Lorain Portrait of Helen Steiner Rice"; previously given to me by Lambert Fitzgerald back in 1999, recalling his words, "Use this image for promoting Helen, the city of Lorain or for your own personal use."

I have always encouraged the free replication, with no "copyright" concerns regarding the use of this particular image, especially in Lorain, and internationally as well. Many local organizations such as the Lorain Public Library and Black River Historical Society have chosen to utilize this "Lorain Portrait" of Helen. The Lakeview Park Ohio Bi-Centennial Historical marker cost $2,000.00 and was dedicated in 2003 with 70 in attendance. It meant so much to me, personally that my brother, Bob and his wife, Mary, drove up from Columbus, just to be supportive. I personally donated $1,000.00, to help pay for the marker. Additionally, I wrote and received two $500.00 grants from both the Longaberger Basket Company and the Ohio Historical Society in Columbus, respectfully. (Helen has state recognition in Columbus, Dayton and Cincinnati.)

I also then personally paid, along with some of the FHSR treasury monies, for rose bushes at the dedication of the Lorain Lakeview Rose Garden, in memory of both Mr. and Mrs. Richard Knitter after their deaths, in gratitude for their dedication, service to Helen's legacy, our society, and their Christian fellowship. Then I bought another rose bush in honor of Helen Steiner Rice at Lakeview, the premier public park of Lorain. Our treasury, for the first ten years, was always rather meager as membership was typically around five members for the first five years of our existence. Today, about 22 years later in 2021, we have about $5,000 in our treasury, and almost 30 members.

HISTORY OF THE "INTERNATIONAL WRITERS ASSOCIATION"

In April of 2006, the Friends of Helen Steiner Rice sponsored a book signing and readings ceremony at Lakeview, near the HSR Historic Ohio Bicentennial marker. The event was held in honor of the 25th Anniversary of Helen Steiner Rice's Death (1981). Twenty-nine poets, writers and authors attended. The event was so enthusiastically received, that a goodly portion of those in attendance wanted us to become a writer's support society. We agreed to meet at the Lorain Public Library on June 17, 2006 and while there launched our next significant step: to morph the Friends of Helen Steiner Rice in to the writers group known henceforth as the International Writers Association! Lorain's "nickname" was "The International City" because of our long-standing diversity of citizenry. [See The Morning Journal, April 24, 2006 front page.]

That same summer, I approached Lorain Metro Parks at Lakeview and asked the director Dan Martin if Metro Parks might consider renaming the remodeled "Bath House" the "Helen Steiner Rice Community Center." Even though, I had collected a petition with 750 signatures for that to happen, it did not. Dan loved the idea but detractors wanted the building to be named for Mayor Leonard Moore, the mayor who purchased the lakeside property for Lorain. Other names were also suggested, but Dan did not want conflict and it was, sadly never named for anyone. I had even given the Lorain Portrait of Helen to Mr. Martin that it might be placed above the Fireplace in the upper assembly room. Dan called me to say he was returning the portrait to me, and he brought it back to my home with his apologies. [The Morning Journal, July 20, 2006, pg. B-1, "Meeting gives look at park's future", by Kate Giammarise.]

Charter members, supporting our newly established writers (IWA) society then included: Dr. Mary Hilaire Tavenner, Joyce Ruf Rhodes, (her husband, Bobby Rhodes volunteered to create an IWA website; Al Thiery, Helen Tisler, Holly McCain and Robert Moore enthusiastically supported our new name and our very ambitious goals. These same individuals have been exceptionally faithful to IWA/FHSR. Our beloved Helen Tisler died from Covid in 2020 at the age of 100; our loss, and heaven's gain. Helen Tisler and Al Theiry were two of only three IWA members to be voted "lifelong" members before health concerns prevented their faithful attendance and participation, after years of faithful support. A new Constitution would now be written, strongly based upon the previous composed Constitution, composed for the "Friends of Helen Steiner Rice."

While serving the Faith Followers, I wrote letters to the Lorain School Board asking them to name a school in Helen's honor. I also attended a School Board meeting in person to make this request personally; all to no avail. I created petitions to honor HSR with a street, another for a building, and still another for a park in Lorain to bear her name, but it all came to nothing until 2007, when I. personally gathered the signatures of 1,000 local residents and voters of Lorain to name a Lorain school after Helen. I then delivered these names to the Lorain City School Board, whereby, shortly thereafter, called and told that a new elementary school in Lorain would be built on Tacoma Avenue in South Lorain and named "Helen Steiner Rice Elementary" on February 26, 2007. The school was built and finished by August 27, 2007, and the dedication ceremony was held the following year, with about five IWA/FHSR members proudly attending.

By now, our group was becoming our newly shared vision and purpose, that of continuing to keep the legacy of Helen forefront, but now, additionally: to help our local writers to obtain a collective voice in our local community, regarding their talents and passion for the written word. In time, we discovered members were joining from Buffalo, NY, Indiana, Kentucky, and throughout the state of Ohio. We continued to average three to six members who would attend" in person" our monthly meetings, routinely held at the Lorain Public Library. "On the books", early on, we did have about twenty registered/paying members. Because our membership had so few members attending, in person, to the monthly library gatherings, Dr. Tavenner proposed quarterly meetings and found attendance now tripled. At that time (July of 2011), we had 27 active (paying $10.00 annual dues) members and generally about fifteen of them would attend the quarterly meetings: the third Saturday in February, May, August and November. [The Morning Journal, "Spotlight", Winter edition, 2010, Pg. 4-7, by Ron Vidika.]

In August of 2011, upon a second renewal of our "non-profit corporation status" in the great state of Ohio, our official name was officially changed by voting membership to: The International Writers Association/Friends of Helen Steiner Rice. This was done in order to embrace our humble beginnings and our "collective vision" for our future.

Our volunteer officers were and remained in office until "official elections" took place." Dr. Tavenner, President; Robert Moore, Vice-President; Denise McKee, Secretary and Joyce Ruf Rhodes, Treasurer. Over the years, we observed that about 50 percent of those who joined our society would choose to stay active and remain supportive of our mutual/ongoing/collective goals, events and vision. Bobby Rhodes and James O. Barnes created the official logo of IWA/FHSR. Bobby Rhodes had created our first IWA/FHSR website. Richard Todd created a second and most impressive website, promoting our writers society locally, nationally and internationally. By 2012, Richard was reporting as many as 20,000 annual hits to our site! In time, this brought us a number of members from outside of the United States. [The Morning Journal, "Celebrate Helen Steiner Rice's 112th Birthday this Saturday", Pg. B-1, May 17, 2012, by Bill Delaney.]

THE NORTHEAST OHIO CHRISTIAN WRITERS CONFERENCE

In the year, 2013, the first weekend of April, Kelly Boyer Sagert, newly elected Treasurer, and James O. Barnes, talented member, led a group of IWA/FHSR members, Robert Moore, Debbie Alferio and Richard Todd, with the critical financial support of IWA, to hold the First Annual Northeast Ohio Christian Writers Conference at Presbyterian Heritage Church in Amherst. After James O. Barnes left IWA/FHSR, Kelly continued to lead and moderate the very successful NEOCWC until 2018 when Kelly then asked Dr. Tavenner to become the Chair to organize the April, 2019 Conference, which she agreed to do. With the help of IWA membership, LCCC, the Lorain Rotary and IWA/FHSR membership, the 7th Annual Northeast Ohio Christian Writers Conference was successfully held, with 57 writers attending. Attendance, during the seven years, has vacillated from 40 to 80 attendees, but the positive reputation of the NEOCWC event has continued to grow over the years. The IWA/FHSR Planning Committee re-located the venue for the 8th Annual Northeast Ohio Christian Writers Conference to the Lorain County Community College Learning Center, downtown Lorain and IWA/FHSR continues to support and staff this very academic conference for, mostly our membership and other local writers

As years would pass, we would agree to a variety of scheduled meetings, depending on membership and need.. New membership has brought even greater talent and it needs to be noted that James O. Barnes has created his own publishing company as well as a Northeast Ohio Christian Writers Conference with the help of other very active members such as Kelly Boyer Sagert, Robert Moore, Debbie Alferio and Richard Todd. IWA always supported this writer conference, fiscally and in every other manner, professionally held for six years at the Presbyterian Heritage Church in Amherst. The event continues to expand and has been excelled, by all measures.

In April, 2014, James O. Barnes held our first official IWA/FHSR elections whereby active members voted. The results were as follows: President: Dr. Tavenner; Vice-President, Robert Moore; Secretary: Denise McKee; Treasurer: Kelly Boyer Sagert. James agreed (God bless him!) to oversee future elections.

At the Lorain County Community College City Center downtown Lorain location, during May of 2015, IWA/FHSR was invited to the LCCC Learning Center by Dina Ferrer, Director, to have a ceremony marking the 115th anniversary of Helen Steiner Rice's birthday! It was well attended by locally elected officials, people from Helen Steiner Rice's church, Lighthouse Methodist, the press, even 4 devoted "fans" of HSR from Reedsville Pennsylvania, as well as a variety of local citizens from Lorain, Amherst, Vermillion and Elyria! Approximately 70 people were in attendance. IWA/FHSR authors had an opportunity to sell books and Charlene Connors, a highly respected and devoted IWA member, performed, "in costume", a most informative and enlightening portrayal of Helen Steiner Rice for all present! Great reviews! [Elyria Chronicle-Telegram, "Helen Steiner Rice fete May 17", pg. B3, May 1, 2015, by Christina Jolliffe.] [Lorain Morning Journal, "Lorain-area writers honor poet Helen Steiner Rice", Front page, May 18, 2015, by Richard Payerchin.] [Lorain Morning Journal, EDITORIAL,"Steiner Rice's Advice remains relevant today", pg.A-7, May 24, 2015.]

The new website has continued to bring writers to IWA from outside of the USA; places such as: India, Scotland, Cayman

Islands, China, Viet Nam, Nigeria, etc. As previously stated, it is a real challenge to keep these writers served and engaged in our Lorain, OH writers society! Richard Todd continues to serve IWA exceptionally with his skills and efforts as our extremely appreciated "Website Administrator".

A DECADE LATER

In February of 2016, Lambert Fitzgerald, brother-in-law to Helen Steiner Rice, composed, certified and made copies of a letter stating that any citizen of Lorain County or organization has the right to teach, speak of, promote or write about Helen Steiner Rice. This certified letter is an important document as some of us had gotten the impression from Cincinnati that the Helen Steiner Rice Foundation has ALL rights to Helen. No one else could write or publish aspects of her life journey. The biography, <u>Ambassador of Sunshine</u> could NEVER have been produced without the generosity and magnanimous sharing of Helen's personal effects by Lambert with the HSR Foundation.. The document, in no way, clearly does not afford anyone or any group in Cincinnati as having "a copyright on the life and legacy" of HSR. Copies of Lambert's letter were distributed to IWA/FHSR members at a library meeting.

In 2016, our members decided that we needed to return to monthly meetings once again! There are so many events and issues of concern, that after 17 years, it appears the decision to have been a wise one. At our June 18th meeting, our IWA/FHSR society and the public marked 10 years since IWA "was born" in 1999. It was on April 23, 2016 that The Friends of Helen Steiner Rice and our local community celebrated the 25th anniversary of Helen Steiner Rice's death on April 23, 1981 at Lakeview Park.

The following month, on Saturday, June 18, 2016, IWA/FHSR met in the Rotary Pavilion near the Helen Steiner Rice Historical Bicentennial Marker to honor local writers and the writing profession.

Some of the speakers included: Kelly Boyer Sagert, Robert Moore, Melba Asberry, Teresa Linden, Miranda Garganz, Julie (Holly) McCain, me and others. Because there was an open microphone, numerous other brave souls addressed the group as well. Local authors could sell their books, and refreshments were shared. It proved to be another "landmark" gathering for locally talented writers!

On October 8, 2016 the Lorain Public Library hosted an Independent Authors event. (Indie Authors)Valerie Smith, Lorain librarian over saw the event, and ten IWA/FHSR attended. Because this was the first ever, national attempt at supporting independent (self-published) authors, the experience was novel to say the least! Very few of our books were sold, and a national panel of speakers along with a locally assembled panel presented their individual thoughts and insights. Valerie Smith asked IWA to assume a leadership role in the 2nd annual October, 2017 "Indie Author" event. But that never materialized as Valerie Smith retired.

After 17 years of IWA/FHSR, on December 17th, we enjoyed a very brief business meeting in the library so that we could personally celebrate together, sharing the "anniversary" of the Birth of Our Lord, Jesus Christ. It was our first time, ever doing this…serving refreshments and celebrating Christmas together! It was one very memorable gathering for those of us present.

On the first weekend of April of 2019, LCCC, City Center and Dina Ferrer, director, invited IWA to host their 7th Annual Northeast Ohio Christian Writers Conference at the Broadway/W. Erie location. Relocating the conference in 2019 was a very good plan. There would be a significant savings in both the site and the food venue. Sixty-five writers, children as well, attended and the presenters, per usual, were always astute, inspiring and excellent. A committee of three organized the event, but many volunteers made it the success that it truly was. Writers especially and always appreciated a venue for selling their books. Dina and her staff could not have been more gracious. [The Senior Years, Lorain County Office on Aging, April 2019, Vol. 45. No.4, pg. 3.]

On November 9, 2019, the Lorain Historical Society held a Helen Steiner Rice Exhibit Preview which featured artifacts and archival materials of Helen's estate at the Moore House, 309 W. 5th Street. That program lasted an hour and so worth every minute. Quite a few of HSR fans attended.

On May 19, 2019, IWA/FHSR enthusiastically planned and scheduled a Memorial Remembrance Service at the Gravesite of Helen Steiner Rice, her parents and sister, Gertrude at Elmwood Cemetery. Approximately 20 people joined IWA/FHSR's remembrance of Helen, on what was the 119th anniversary of her birth in Lorain, OH. I composed "Ten Things We Should Know about Helen Steiner Rice" and IWA members read them aloud for the attending public. Both the Elyria Chronicle Telegram and the Lorain Morning Journal attended and published wonderful articles. We were especially delighted to welcome Mary Springkowski, Lorain Councilwoman-at-large and her husband to our public gathering. [The Morning Journal, April 28.2019, pg. A-3.] [The Morning Journal, May 20, 2019, pg. A-2., Richard Payerchin.] [Elyria Chronicle-Telegram, May 20, 2019, pg. C-1, Bruce Walton.]

On Sunday, September 15th, the director of Ridge Hill Memorial Park held a very impressive 90 Year Community Memorial Celebration. (1929-2019). Dr. Tavenner was invited to speak at the Praying Hands Niche Memorial in honor of Helen Steiner Rice. Hundreds attended the event that day as more than 24,000 people are interred at Ridge Hill; almost 4,000 of them are Veterans. Numerous speakers were employed that day sharing an array of topics. The celebration could not have been more eventful! I welcomed the gathering and led the group in prayer, but employed the assistance of attendee volunteers to read aloud, individually for all present, her composition "Ten Things All Should Know About Helen Steiner Rice". A word of warning to the reader...this is a summary of the first half of this book...Helen's life journey. You may or may not wish to review!

TEN THINGS ALL SHOULD KNOW ABOUT HELEN STEINER RICE

1. Helen Elaine Steiner was born to Anna Bieri and John Steiner. Anna and her family were from Switzerland. John Steiner was of German descent; both met and married in Kettering, OH. After marrying, Mr. Steiner got a job with the Baltimore and Ohio Railway and the couple moved to Lorain, OH where Helen was born on May 19, 1900. A year and a half later, on November 2, 1902, Gertrude, Helen's only sibling, was born, as was Helen, in the home that Anna and John had rented at 1939 Lexington Avenue. This building is currently on the list of houses to be demolished in Lorain.

2. Later, Helen's parents built their own home built at 2714 Reid Avenue. The family continued to worship at the nearby 20th Street Methodist Church. It eventually relocated to Meister Rd. and was renamed Christ United Methodist. In the 1980's and after merging with several other churches, the name was changed once again and is now known as the Lorain Lighthouse Methodist Church.

3. Both Helen and Gertrude attended Garden Avenue Elementary, Garfield, and Lorain High Schools. Helen was very involved in her church. She taught Bible school there and had thoughts of becoming a preacher. At Lorain

High School, she seriously considered attending Ohio Wesleyan College, becoming a lawyer, and then perhaps a Congresswoman, but after a few months after her high school graduation, her father died in the 1918 Spanish Influenza Pandemic. It killed as many as 60 million people world-wide. Helen was grateful to obtain a much-needed job at Lorain Electric Light and Power Company.

4. After a few very productive years, Helen decided to start her own company, "Steiner Service" where her talents as a gifted poet and public speaker led her, at the age of 27, into a very successful career. She spoke throughout the United States and was even invited to the White House to meet and be photographed with President Calvin Coolidge. Her speaker's fee, at today's rate, would be several thousand dollars. After presenting a speech to the Dayton Savings and Bank in Dayton, OH, Helen met Mr. Franklin Rice, whom she married in New York City six months later, at the age of 28. They bought a 14 room house in Dayton, complete with three cars!

5. Shortly after their honeymoon cruise in the Caribbean, in the fall of 1929, the NY Stock Market crashed. Their fortune was depleted and in 1931, after Franklin lost his job at the bank, Helen was fortunate to obtain a position in Cincinnati at the Gibson Art Company through a good friend. Franklin refused to move from their home in Dayton, so Helen commuted back and forth from Cincinnati every weekend. After several years of financial struggle, Franklin was so depressed and overwhelmed by their financial losses, that on October 14, 1932, he committed suicide. He went into their garage, turned on the car engine, and closed the garage doors. Helen buried her husband of three years in a nearby cemetery in Moraine, OH, in the Rice family plot. Helen then sold their home and permanently moved to Cincinnati, building an extremely successful career with her gift for rhyme, and was soon promoted to Editor of Verse.

6. Helen enjoyed loving and family-like relationships in Cincinnati while living at the Gibson Hotel. In 1945, her mother died unexpectedly of a heart attack. After that, Helen commuted to Lorain from Cincinnati every holiday to be with her sister, Gertrude. They wrote to each other daily. In 1960, some of Helen's poetry was read by Aladdin Palante on the Lawrence Welk Show. This gave her national exposure and when President Kennedy was assassinated, Mr. Welk called Helen at the Reid Street home and asked her to write a poem about this unforeseen tragedy, trying to help America to deal with this stunning event.

7. At the age of 70, after nearly 40 years of service at Gibson Art Company, in the greeting card business, Helen retired because of arthritis and several other health issues. She kept her office there and continued to work at Gibson, but not for money; instead, as she would say, "Now, I work for God." Only a few years later, it was decided to demolish the Gibson Hotel, Helen's home for 40 years, and this seriously impacted her fragile health. She moved less than a mile away into the Cincinnati Club, but lost 30 pounds, and discs in her back had deteriorated, forcing her to wear a brace.

8. On April 23, 1980, Helen fell and broke her left hip and wrist. Consequently, she moved into a Catholic nursing home near Cincinnati. President Jimmy Carter and wife, Rosalyn, as well as Pope John Paul II and hundreds of others sent their get well cards and supportive prayers. On March 14, 1981,the President of Mount St. Joseph College on the Ohio, Sr. Jean Patrice Harrington, a St. Elizabeth Ann Seton Sister of Charity, presented Helen with an Honorary Doctorate of Humane Letters. This was the only degree Helen ever received other than her Lorain High School diploma.

9. On the evening of April 23, 1981, at the age of 80, Helen died at the Franciscan Catholic Nursing Home in

Wyoming, OH. Her body was brought back to Lorain and buried at Elmwood Cemetery, next to the graves of her mother and father. Twelve years later, Gertrude, her dearest friend and sister, was buried next to her. During her lifetime, Helen had published ten hard-cover books of her poetry, and after her death, another 63 books of poems were published. Helen Elaine Steiner Rice is believed to be the most prolific American poet, and possibly the most prolific poet of all times. She thought that she may have written about two million poems. Her spiritual messages and prayerful words continue to be admired, shared and enjoyed throughout the English speaking world. American Greetings headquarters, now located in Westlake, Ohio, bought Helen's greeting card verses from JR Gibson when it closed in Cincinnati. Helen died a millionaire but before she died, her dearly beloved friend Fred Bauer, and former editor of Guide Post Magazine, advised her to establish an estate foundation in her own name. This Helen Steiner Rice Foundation could and would then distribute Helen's sizeable fortune (well over a million dollars) to people with financial needs living within both Lorain and Hamilton Counties after her death. Helen's two respective churches of worship, in both Cincinnati and Lorain, continue to receive financial help even to this day. Believe it or not, the IRS questioned Helen's finance report because they had never known of any individual as wealthy as Helen, so utterly magnanimous with her fortune sharing it with her designated institutions of faith.

10. Helen died 40 years ago. It was over 20 years ago, on December 12, 1999, that four Lorainites gathered at the home of Dick and Betty Knitter to establish the *Friends of Helen Steiner Rice*, a society established to keep Helen's memory alive in her hometown. Two of the founding members, Mr. and Mrs. Knitter, who have since died, knew and loved Helen. The other two founding members are

Helen's brother-in-law, married to Helen's sister, Gertrude, Lambert Fitzgerald, and fellow Lorainite, Dr. Mary Hilaire (Sally) Tavenner. The group continued to work so that Helen, who is recognized around the world, would be remembered and honored in the town she so very much loved, her hometown of Lorain! Lambert has most graciously entrusted all of Helen's personal effects to his good friend, Al Harsar who serves at the Lorain Historical Society. Mr. Harsar has placed all of these treasures in the care of the Lorain Historical Society. Dr. Tavenner continues to serve as the President of the International Writers Association/ Friends of Helen Steiner Rice. This original group of four has grown over the past 20 years to 63 members, and is now represented in 10 different countries. In 2003, The Friends of Helen Steiner Rice designed, dedicated and obtained, for the price of $2,000, an Ohio Bicentennial Historical Marker. With the permission of City Hall, the marker was proudly planted in Lakeview Park. In 2007, the Friends of Helen Steiner Rice were solely responsible for getting the Lorain School Board to name a newly constructed school to be named in her honor. Helen Steiner Rice Elementary School is located in South Lorain on Tacoma Avenue. It was after 7 years of focused effort to get Helen honored in her hometown, the membership of the Friends of Helen Steiner Rice decided to morph into and to actually become the "International Writers Association/Friends of Helen Steiner Rice". The IWA/FHSR is also responsible for holding, annually, each April, the "Annual Northeast Ohio Christian Writers Conferences". In April of 2021, these writers plan to hold the 8th Annual NEOCWC. Dr. T. recently submitted a nomination for Helen to be featured on a US Postage Stamp; certainly a worthy candidate for such consideration. Sadly, the proposal was rejected, but we were told to "try again in eight years"!

WINDING DOWN

—◦◦◦—

There is so very much to share, but I want this second publication of "<u>A Portrait of Helen Steiner Rice: A Lorain Version</u>" to be reasonably brief. I am of the opinion that more people will purchase and read this book, if it remains concise and precise. It is being published so that more souls will be aware of Helen's profound influence during her nearly 81 years among us. Please allow me to speak of 2020 and some of 2021, as the International Writers Association/Friends of Helen Steiner Rice enters its third decade.

In April of 2020, the 8th Annual NEOCWC at LCCC was scheduled for the first weekend of April in 2020. After months of planning and preparation, it had to be cancelled because of Covid-19, a pandemic from Wuhan, China that had invaded and was seriously infecting the world. So our 2020 conference had to be cancelled.

Membership, **before Covid-19 arrived**, for IWAFHSR, was about 63 members in 13 different nations and several US States. The Schedule for in-person IWA meetings was also cancelled. The library was closed and as of May, 2021, no groups may gather there.

Our fellowship and shared values have been strong through the years. I am sure that gathering informally has been a good collective decision. Over the years, IWA has socialized, both individually and collectively, at the family camp of Kelly Boyer Sagert in Medina. We also gathered upon the generous invitation of Judy Kean, at Judy Kean's "Creative Space" Art Studio in Avon Lake on Sept. 19, 2018. On August 17, 2019, IWA held another social with our family and friends at the newly refurbished Century Park Harbor House on the Eastside of Lorain. All of our get-togethers have been enjoyable. Socializing is not just helpful for family members, neighborhoods and communities, but obviously important for most every group of like-minded individuals. Since our gathering of about 50 in August of 2019, Century Park has been given over to the Lorain Metro Parks. Previously, the "East Side" Block Watch group of individuals and volunteers had constructively remodeled both the park and Harbor House. Recently Lorain County Parks have taken over management and care of Century Park.

Covid 19 may have cancelled our 2020 Northeast Ohio Christian Writers Conference and our "in person" meeting sat the library but our very "tech-savvy" current Vice-President, Robert Moore and Treasurer, James O. Barnes found some much needed solutions. We began ZOOM conferencing. On Friday evening, April 9, 2021 and April 10, 2021, we held our FIRST EVER Virtual Northeast Ohio Christian Writers Conference! About 30 writers participated, and we all agreed that the event was both exceptional and extremely successful.

As you can well imagine, it was countless hours of preparation, and the planning committee unanimously decided that James would lead the way, and Robert would be his partner. The conference planning committee: J. Holly Mc Cain, Shirley Gilreath and Dr. Tavenner merely followed their lead. Webmaster, Richard Todd made much of our transition both possible and smooth for all who joined in! There really ARE some amazingly talented members in this writers support group.

However, let it also be known, that due to so many changes over the past year and a half…Covid-19, no "personal contact" due to wearing masks and quarantine requirements, membership has been reduced by more than 50%. To date, as of December 28, 2021, we have only 33 paid IWA members. What will 2022 bring? Your guess is as good as mine!

Yes, The Friends of Helen Steiner Rice 1999-2006 morphed into the International Writers Association and ALL of this began on December 12, 1999. In 2019, a very active and constructive year,

IWA/FHSR commemorated 20 YEARS of service and support to those who enjoy the gift of words, employing the aid of both pen and paper and/or our various and current other new technologies.

We did approach the Director of the Lorain Public Library, asking that they name one of their various rooms (Room A, B, or C) in honor of Helen. We were very sure that would happen, especially after Helen's estate had donated $5,000.00 to the Lorain Public Library. The proposal was rejected by the current Administration.

As 2020 unfolded before us, we could not and did not anticipate many serious changes to come. Because of the arrival of Wuhan Pandemic: Covid-19, so very much changed throughout our nation, and throughout our world. More than 800,000 Americans died due to the Covid Virus.

IN CLOSING

In about twenty pages, we shared with you, the 80 year life of a world-famous talent, and in about twenty more pages, we shared twenty-some years of remembrance. I recall that when I graduated from Lorain High School, 55 years ago, we would usually write on the back of our senior year pictures, while jotting some message, the letters RMA. It was our way of saying to the kids we grew up with and learned to love to please, "Remember Me, Always". I think it in innate desire of many. That is why, perhaps, so many of us obtain a memorial stone for our graves, name our children after us, take family photos, often placing them in albums, and proudly share a family last name. Perhaps, that is why we have a NEW TESTAMENT… that we may never forget Christ or his witness, legacy, teachings, example. The OLD TESTAMENT puts the coming of Christ among us into context, so this writings of both testaments are so utterly relevant. It is natural that we might remember the past and how we got to the moment of time, our present, where we find and live our journeys…

I have recorded the life of Helen as briefly as I could. There was so much more I could say, but I felt, if I keep things brief, maybe more of you would read her story. And if I kept the aftermath of our local societies brief, you would be more prone to read them as well. It was not easy for me to work so hard these past 28 years to get Helen's hometown to pay her the respect due to her many significant accomplishments.

I know some of your heroes may be from the fields of sports, engineering, science, history, politics, music, television or movie "stars" etc. We are all so very different. That is as it should be. My heroes are those who inspire me to become someone greater than I would have been, had I not known them or "their legacies". Helen Steiner Rice is one of those souls. I cannot forget so many extraordinary people I learn of or have met…such as my parents, grandparents, family, friends, St. Mother Teresa of Calcutta (4 times) and St. Pope John Paul IInd (once in Puerto Rico).

Another closing story: One day in early March of 2021, a friend, Dennis Flores, told me that he was on his way to City Hall during our phone conversation. Dennis had been our Councilman Representative in the Ward Two. He worked hard for the families he represented. It came to my mind to ask Dennis, "Will you see Nancy Greer?" He answered, "I plan on it." Nancy is a secretary at City Hall who has served all of our citizens for many years. "Will you ask her if there is any way we might get the Mayor of Lorain (Jack Bradley) to proclaim April 23rd, Helen Steiner Rice Day for Lorain? Helen died 40 years ago on April 23, 1981 and I thought this would be a befitting remembrance. (Such proclamations had happened in years past, Former Mayor Olejko once proclaimed Helen's birthday, May 19th, "Helen Steiner Rice" before I returned to Lorain, years ago, and so this was not a precedent, by any means. It was just an additional "celebration of appreciation for Helen's life journey".)

Nancy liked the idea and sent the idea forward with Breanna Dull to the Mayor's Secretary, Paula Tooney. All of them were in unison and when the Mayor was approached, he too, felt it was a great idea. They offered to present the proclamation to me…but I had a much better recipient in mind: the Pastor of Helen's Congregation: Lorain Lighthouse United Methodist Church. (Helen's Congretation) My cousins, Becky and Chuck Boals have spent many years serving in this church and knew the pastor as a friend. I asked them to ask Rev. Adam Davis if he was willing to accept the proclamation from the Mayor. He enthusiastically accepted the invitation.

I was given permission to compose and distribute a press release to numerous sources of media. It read as follows

On Friday, April 23, 2021....Mayor Jack Bradley will proclaim this day "HELEN STEINER RICE DAY" because it was 40 years ago on April 23, 1981, that Helen died. The Mayor took his Proclamation to Helen's Congregation, the Lorain Lighthouse United Methodist Church, 3015 Meister Rd, Lorain, 44053 and presented it to the pastor, Rev. Adam M. Davis, at 2:00 pm. Due to Covid concerns, the event took place outside of the church, in the parking lot. About 30 supporters were in attendance.

In review, Lorain has honored Helen's memory often, naming a public school in Helen's honor, placing and dedicating an Ohio Bicentennial Historical Marker, recognizing her life, near the Rotary Pavilion at Lakeview Park and many events have been held over the past 40 years, all accomplished as a tribute to Helen's legacy. Helen was an inspirational poet who "may have" composed as many as a million poems. We do know that Helen died a millionaire, and left much of her estate to Lorain County Center for Children and Youth Services, Center for Visually Impaired, El Centro, Lorain County Community College, Lorain County Free Clinic, Lorain County Lutheran/Presbyterian Ministry, Inc., Sacred Heart Chapel (Youth Development Program), Christ United Methodist, now: Lighthouse United Methodist, Lorain Public Library and many other Lorain County societies. Helen's estate has been distributed in both Lorain and Hamilton Counties. Much of her "personal estate" is currently in Lorain Historical Society. [The Morning Journal, Front page: April 24, 2021 "Poet Helen Steiner Rice Honored" by Richard Payerchin.] [The Chronicle-Telegram, Front page: April 24, 2021, "Helen Steiner Rice Honored" by Carissa Woytach.]

There were about 30 individuals in attendance, wearing masks and in the parking lot; a variety of faiths and denominations. We felt a communal joy while witnessing and participating in the celebration. I have been blessed to have shared in so many remembrances of Helen over the past 30 years. I am certain there are more to come.

The following day, I received a phone call from Catherine Miceli. I had no idea who this lady was, but she explained that she read the story of the Proclamation in the Lorain Journal and wanted to speak with me. Catherine lived across the street from Gertrude and because Helen was such a frequent visitor, came to know both sisters extremely well. The Miceli household would share rhubarb, vegetables and corn from their garden. Helen would, in turn, give Catherine's three children and her mother gifts of gratitude. Catherine told me that she will turn 97 on May 22nd of this year.

Helen especially enjoyed the home made "Lady Locks" that Catherine's mother would make, and once sent her secretary (Mary Jo Eling) from Cincinnati to Lorain to get a box of the home made "delectables". Catherine and I probably spoke for an hour and I found her stories so very interesting! What a "personal touch" I felt from Helen throughout our conversation! Imagine that, after Lorain honors Helen at her Lorain Parish Congregation, Lighthouse United Methodist Church just the day before our talk, Helen's still-living and still-very loving neighbor went to her phone book to find my number for a very delightful conversation! It was all so impressive.

Three years ago, the Lorain Schools Alumni Association Inc. organized a "Alumni Hall of Fame" for any Lorainite who may have graduated from any High School in Lorain: Lorain Steelmen, Southview Saints, Admiral King, Lorain Catholic Spartans, St. Mary's High School. Nominees are submitted at least 15 years after having graduated.

The inductees are elected by a volunteer committee because of one or more of the following factors: academic excellence; for arts/cultural enrichment; business acumen; career achievement; community leadership; heroism; humanitarianism; health/wellness; and/or philanthropy. Last year, I nominated Helen Steiner Rice and she was selected. Because of this, I was invited to the June 26, 2021 Induction Ceremony at the Lorain Shipyards. About 100 attended. After an opening prayer, we all partook of a most delectable selection of food from the breakfast bar before the official business took place. There were 12 "selected individuals" who were spoken of and plaques presented. Four of the twelve, were deceased; (obviously Helen among them). The Lorain Alumni Association Committee asked me to speak for 5 minutes addressing Helen's legacy. Helen died with over a million dollars, and the money was put in a trust to be shared with many organizations in both Hamilton and Lorain Counties. That is impressive philanthropy. Twelve men and women also constituted the Association Committee, and they, collectively, provided a most impressive and inspiring 3 hour long program.

It was excruciating to speak for 5 minutes about Helen. Actually impossible, but I let the people understand why it was impossible for me to do this. There are just far too many significant accomplishments, and too many noteworthy aspects of Helen's life journey.

Helen Steiner Rice: A Lorain Portrait cannot be effectively shared in five minutes. I am proud to report that there have been many celebrations, memorials, remembrances and gatherings over the past nearly 30 years that I have been privy to, and so many more, throughout multiple Ohio cites as well as in other states and communities.

For example, Jessica Mowery Foster, from Reedsville, PA came to Lorain with her grandparents, Mr. and Mrs. Schaaf numerous times to learn more about Helen. Jess even portrayed Helen while attending Indian Valley High School. I was able to visit Reedsville several times as well...to attend Jessica's High School graduation, and her wedding. (On the back of Jess and Ed's wedding program, Aug. 29, 2015, they published Helen's poem: "The Magic of Love". I am delighted to say, we may live a many miles apart, but have remained very connected for nearly the past two decades to this remarkable family! [The Sentinel, Lewistown, PA, January 10, 2009, pg. D-7, Micaniah Wise Bilger.]

I still have every hope to see the National Women's Hall of Fame accept Helen Steiner Rice as an inductee. Lately, I have watched (even attended) many very liberal, far left candidates being accepted and consequently, honored. I have, personally nominated Helen at least 10 times, and know others who have tried as well. At the Seneca Falls, New York, National Women's Hall of Fame, some of us would love to plan a bus trip from Ohio to the Installation of Helen in 2023. Please allow me to encourage you to ALSO nominate Helen and use the content of this book to help you. One of our International Writers Association Writers in Texas assures me that she is planning to do exactly that. Simply go to: www.womenofthehall.org to get the online application. It matters not who gets through to these judges; only that it happens.

Really, there is just no way that I can record in this very condensed version of Helen's life impelling my passion (Part Two) for her extraordinary talent and influence within my soul. I have given many talks on Helen's life-journey, and have published numerous articles, but so have many of her other followers. I just cannot tell you everything in fifty pages! (Please visit my website: www.dutchink.com to learn more.) I have not even mentioned that American Greetings Headquarters near Cleveland bought all the rights to Helen's most lucrative collection of greeting cards, first sold by Gibson in Cincinnati. American Greetings bought the rights to publish and sell Helen's cards after Gibson in Cincinnati closed. Helen's talent continues to inspire and touch lives, not just "back in her day".

My prayer and hope is that many will purchase this "book" to read and to share with others as a gift. Not just in Lorain, but throughout the world, because Helen did impact our nation and our world in such a godly, positive manner. I hope you found all of this to be somewhat interesting. That is exactly what every writer hopes when they write for his/her readers. I thank you for sharing your time with me. This has been a labor of love.

I want to finish with a few of Helen's words. This is something she had enclosed in one of her very many letters: "Although I have been away from Lorain for over 25 years, I still have a warm feeling of fondness and gratitude in my heart for the spot I am still proud to call MY HOME TOWN."

SOURCES

--------•⊙(⦿)•--------

For more information about Helen Steiner Rice contact your local library. Currently, much of Helen's personal letters, photographs and effects are being housed in the Lorain Historical Society. Lambert Fitzgerald, Helen's brother-in-law entrusted them to Al Harsar who recently placed them, for now, in the Lorain Historical Society.

Sources used for the writing of these articles include: *In the Vineyard of the Lord* as told to Fred Bauer; published by F.H. Revell, Old Tappan, New Jersey, © 1979; Helen S. Rice—Ambassador of Sunshine by Ronald Pilitt & Virginia Wiltse; published by Guideposts, Carmel, New York, © 1994; "This I Believe" by HSR; the vertical file of the Lorain Public Library, Lorain, Ohio 44053, the Lorain Historical Society which has shared many of Helen's personal collection of invaluable correspondence bequeathed to her sister, Gertrude, then to her brother-in-law, Lambert Fitzgerald. Much of this information was also taken from the archives of The Friends of Helen Steiner Rice/International Writers Association, 1999-2022.

AFTERWORD

I encourage Americans to continue to explore her poetry. The Friends of Helen Steiner Rice, a society born in 1999, for the purpose of establishing a lasting memorial to Helen's work in her hometown of Lorain, Ohio, and to educate the public about her life and legacy became the springboard for the International Writers Association.

After 7 years, members of the Friends of Helen Steiner Rice had managed to get a Lorain City School named in Helen's honor, and an Ohio Bicentennial Historical Marker dedicated to Helen in placed in Lorain's premier public park, "Lakeview". Many of these people were writers and asked if we could morph into a writer's society. We renamed "The Friends of Helen Steiner Rice" to "The International Writers Association". Check out the IWA/FHSR website at www.internationalwritersassociation.com. Membership for IWA/FHSRS is $25.00. Pay on PayPal on our website or mail your check (no cash please) to our Treasurer, in care of International Writers Association 121 N. Leavitt Rd. Ste. 125, Amherst, OH 44001

I will recommend you read the "vertical file" at the Lorain Public Library, or research stories in both the Lorain Journal and Elyria Chronicle. The Lorain Historical Society has a priceless treasure trove of information. I am not sure how many of you will care to explore these resources, but they are available.

Helen was a fascinating woman, who lived a most productive, remarkable, adventurous life. As you know, she once estimated that she may have written as many as two million poems during her years. I think the estimate closer to one million, but who is to really know? Do you have the time or desire to count them? I have not. Many of her poems were brief, and even her personal letters were often composed in verse, especially those written for birthdays, weddings, ets. Because Hallmark Greeting Cards have bought the rights for Helen's verses to use on their greeting cards, from Gibson in Cincinnati, OH, they may be another place to do some research. Go to your local library, wherever you may live—see what they have on Helen. Check the "internet". But please, do allow these stories to be what I have hoped them to be: "**a beginning.**"

Lightning Source UK Ltd.
Milton Keynes UK
UKHW051332180223
417122UK00025B/1707